A LIFETIME OF VERSE

SANDRA R. POUND

ISBN 978-1-940645-86-5

COURIER PUBLISHING

Greenville, South Carolina

PRINTED IN THE UNITED STATES OF AMERICA

Dedication

To the memory of my mother, Helen Costie Causey Richardson, who babbled rhyme as easily as breathing. She had a houseful of daughters whom she inspired to be lovers of verse and a son to be a singer and guitar player. She is the reason I think in verse and write some of those thoughts down.

FOREWORD

As a pastor's wife, one of the joys of my life has been becoming acquainted with interesting people along the way. One of the most enjoyable people I've known is Dr. Sandra Pound.

I have been immensely blessed to sit for hours as a guest in her beautiful home as we shared stories and experiences of our life journeys. Although we were both in retirement when our paths crossed, I learned of the many commonalities of our faith, upbringing, and relationships.

Having been introduced to her writings and experiences has further endeared me to her. Beginning with a play, then her compilation of a family history, then her realistic fiction and short stories, I have seen heartfelt reflections of her life and faith.

I am delighted to recommend this collection of poetry. Sandra's talent continues to shine as she writes on a wide variety of life-experiences. As demonstrated in her earlier writings, her voice resounds with her faith.

I would be remiss not to mention her conviction for the salvation of those who are lost and hurting. At the end of the last section of this book, "Poems About God," she explains the way to salvation through Jesus Christ, so that no reader would go forward without knowledge of her Savior and Lord.

Hear Sandra's thought-provoking verse, and enjoy the writing of my friend — and that of a notably talented South Carolina author.

— Connie Hardwick Singleton

TABLE OF CONTENTS

POEMS ABOUT CHILDREN

POEMS ABOUT LIFE, NATURE, AND DEATH

POEMS ABOUT GOD

A LIFETIME OF VERSE

POEMS ABOUT POETRY

Poems

I love
the way
you can
get lost
inside
a poem's
winding
hallway.
You are
inside
the poem
until
you
have read
it
all.
But
after
you have read
it
through,
the poem
is inside of
you.

THE ONE AND ONLY POEM

One day you hear a poem for the very first time and
all of you says, "Wow! I think I love you."
Your heart beats a bit faster. Your palms perspire.
You may even feel the proverbial butterflies in the pit of your stomach.
You know you are changed by the knowledge that this poem exists;
you want to get to know it better.
Is it love at first sight?
Is it infatuation,
— a faulty impression of love —
mere fascination?
Or could it be
the *real* thing?
Love needs time.
You give it time.
Love wants to know every intimate detail —
innuendos, nuances, hints and coy smiles.
You read it and reason it for those
poetic devices, hidden meanings.
Love grows as it learns more.
Love does not turn its back.
Word by line, you internalize —
searching, believing, hoping —
finally trusting. This poem is vital.
In memory, each phrase is a kiss
to muse over again and again
and each stanza a promise
of an endless relationship.
You want others to see it
to know that it is yours.
You own this poem.
It is yours.
Forever.

My Solemn Soul Needs Poetry

and restore my soul.
and similes are sunshine that glows
and imagery, the rain that grows
and words, houses with rooms
where verses are living worlds,

       upward,

       in,

       am

       I

       pit

       the

       of

       out

       me

       pulls

       that

       rope

       the

       is

       poem

       A

The Poet

The poet deposits dear for the future
each day he writes a line.
Each metaphor creates a mother lode
for seeking minds to find a rich vein
from the poet's past that will —
when mined with all one's might —
connect that one to the light
at the end of the tunnel.

The Children Meet in Poetry

He met a child in a poem story
and saw his own reflection
though they did not look a thing alike.
The setting had no similarity
but the poem story child used words
he could have said
had he known the words before
when he had been afraid.
Now the poem words
will come to mind
on the day
he needs
them.
He will have the words to say.

The Songwriter

In the hours of the dawn
I pick up a piece of paper
to place words that will not be silent and gone.
The heart of the matter
is that my heart will not stop yearning to be known —
the words spread out on paper
of a me still waiting to be born.
Songs of life
that have been hidden
or held back or
kicked aside —
they will not die.
They breathe still and a cry arises.
They are the dawn rising up —
they will live
when we are gone.

The Poem

I decided you were the one
when I read the line of the poem
Not because of who you are but
Because of who I am when I'm with you.
And then he whom I'd loved all my life
and waited for
came.
I wonder how it would have played out
except for the line in that poem.

Verses Versus Rejections

The fabric was separating
from the wire that curved around the corners.
Inside,
the precious cargo,
pulled from door to door
over the course of the decades,
thinking someone would invite it in
and understand,
but,
even if they looked and read,
they always shook their head.
She knew she would keep walking
instead of tossing
the whole weary work into a dumpster
because she could not stop
the small voice inside her heart
that turned into cryptic words at dark.
No, in a small font.
But why?
What's the purpose?
No one wants to understand.
They want fresh.
It *was once* fresh and true,
but now it's only true.
The time has passed —
why not allow them to die?
No, the voice whispered.
No, in a bold font.

The Neglected Poems

Let me see,
I think I left them here
on that day of disappointment
and rejection.
It was here I came, I think,
or was it there
I buried it —
the entire bag of them.
If I could but find it still —
the bag with all the verse —
to His name I would rehearse
giving praise and thankfulness.
I would hurry to use the gift —
the gift He allotted me —
by multiplying it —
for
the Master
cometh
quickly.

Facebook Muse

Sure my poetry is like Facebook
fall drifting leaves
yes it is a little lame
in the way of textbooks dictionaries and newspapers
it's the breathing out of nothingness
that fills the world of the air today
the just happening
just thinking
just wondering
of a mind that left the door open
but it is what it is
and it tells my story in a way
that many today
will read and say
yeah man I know.

Musky Poets

He rides majestically endowed
or maybe poorly unnoticed
holding a banner of life word by word
the eternal course
trodden by would-be wordmakers
who strive to ingrain in the mind a heart.
Emily harnessed skillfully and rode
jumping fences with ease and made a
reader say, "Now did you see how
she pulled that off so gracefully —
I almost missed it. Glad I looked back."
Walt sat loosely in the saddle and his
route was wide and open as he did so with minds —
he spoke to the ones that were open.
Frost a gentle gait commanded
questioning close to home.
And poor Poe didn't know which way to go.
But these poets have been long forgotten
except by old English literature teachers
who like the musky smell of the century's old verse.
What is your ride like, young poet?
Does your steed stop to graze twenty-first century viruses
and then like a GPS send you off to other villages of the world
to report injustices
or do you stay close in on the round track of life and love
and write what you know in cryptic words and thoughts?

Poet of Poets

We go back to the poet —
the one who tended sheep
penning words
simple and complete
words about a Greater Shepherd
who loved
and cared
and tended all sheep
all time
everywhere —
when our days are lonely,
sad
when we are fearful
weak.
It is the poet of poets
and the One of whom he speaks —
the Gentle Greater Shepherd —
He is the one we seek.

POEMS ABOUT LOVE

Loud and Sweet

The music in my head
gets louder and will not go away —
bringing a certain sweetness coloring my day.
Uninhibited, I move to its tempo —
staccato-like or sway.
The tantalizing sweetness lingers and tempers
but what amazes me
is how the cadence is so loud!

Paradox Eternal

Like the night
of the day
we are forever
apart.
Yet
in a crystal instant
of lunar solar enterprise —
crisscrossed
entwined —
mine and your stars
crystallized
for all time
and space.

Passions

Pick your passions
carefully, so
you do not lose
yourself on the ephemeral.
With patience
pick your passions, or
they will make
a patient out of you.

Intentionally Untended

The frayed imperfections of my life
I look upon now
as necessary loose ends
I always,
always
meant to savor
for a moment
and then
sever.

But
you —
the frayed midnight
of all my days —
I savored
in silence
and
forgot
to trim away.

THE REMAINDER OF TODAY

What difference does it make if you go or stay
or what kind of car you drive off in anyway?
What difference if you win or lose at games
or how you choose to play?
What difference does it make if your hair is streaked
with expensive gold or naturally with gray?
What difference if you wear those shoes from *that* store
or the worn and faithful flip-flops you so adore?
What difference if you use too much salt on your meat
or always prefer white bread instead of wheat?
What difference if there is no sunshine for weeks
or if rain falls seven days complete?
What difference if you're really happy
or always a shade of blue?
Who really cares about your life —
what you say and do?
Something way down deep inside —
beyond the innermost DNA
of you and me —
some kind of seed —
wants us to grow free —
it whispers for you to keep on keeping on —
there will be tomorrow
and better yet —
the remainder of today
and somewhere, somehow, *someone*
waits and wants you to see
the real won't go away.

BACK TO CAROLINE

Leaves meandering
through the sky
take me back
to Caroline.
They take me back
to Caroline
and to the green grass where we lay
and the beach sand where we played
on those certain summer days
when sunshine warmed our bodies and
we were engulfed in secret smiles.
Promises we made to birds on high —
promises of love that would never die —
promises of never leaving and wondering why —
promises so brave they made us cry.
What color were the leaves sailing through the sky?
What color were the birds that day —
were they red or blue or gray?
I really cannot say.
Arachne world, set me free —
once more April days to see
when mornings were too long
and nights too brief —
when love was too strong
to find relief.
Floating leaves and flying birds
of blue or red or brown or black
take me back
take me back.
Take me back
once more in time and mind
to love like there in Caroline.

Love's Rose

To hold a rose too tightly
will crush it.
If your impassioned hand
with fingers twined resolutely binding
clutch the succulent style
of the budding velvet,
it will long more
to be free.
And if that liberty is not to be,
then dire decay you will see
among the garden's loveliest bloom —
for crushing
surely means its doom.

Harvest Bounty

Like a summer swing
without a passenger
my heart had been
but was now watermelon wafting
on my senses dizzying me with delight!
Not political
not revolutionary
not rights nor wrongs
but pregnant idolatries in senseless warfare
of hungry minds
simple
small
a seed — no
a complicated
gargantuan
elephant of the senses —
you!

Winter of the Heart

That year the trees were stripped
revealing their nakedness
and in a way their honesty beautiful —
pure paleness lying bare.
The only thing was
the vile vulnerability —
the coldness copied on a forever forest
that would never leaf again.
The barest tree, I observed, offered
an empty glass to a horse beneath.
Then spring came again another year
in perfect paleness of what would color in summer
to complete the almanac of my life.
My soul sighted an earth unleashed
sprinkling joys of nature
again,
for me.
Anticipating
stripped of self
nakedness revealing
pale white beauty of
vulnerability
standing before God
like a new bought canvas.

Life Was Day-old Bread

My heart was a dried-up bean
only a trace of what it could have been.
It had starved that way
atrophied
a day at a time
shriveled,
shrunken,
dormant,
dead —
Then
you
came!

POEMS ABOUT MARRIAGE

Lovelorn

As premium as life could offer
two in the past
both bold strong
yearning to belong —
the choice
was wearisome for a heart divided
but time and they compelled.
The one chosen
proved faithful true and brought
children and happy days until
one long summer day
when evening was waiting
a memory arose quite by
an accident of the mind
of the one who had been left behind
of the life that could have been.
Had there been a twist of fate
had there been a grave mistake
had the other one been taken
would my mind not be now shaken?
Or would I be the same as now
looking back wondering how?
The eternal question
do we trust a young heart before time?
Age shows us one is to be left behind
in the shadows of the mind.
We might ponder what we lose
in that moment when we choose —
but somehow know it is true —
no matter what we ever do —
the puzzle will ever come to mind
of what and who we left behind.

I Tried to Hide

I tried to hide
to disappear
in the vastness of you
who loomed consuming
all my thoughts and dreams and coming years.
Is it right and divine to do this —
to be one is to be you?
The will is hard to kill
and I find there is a bit of me
that wants to still live.
I believe that God intended
love to hold us up instead of pull us back
or drown ourselves completely in the other
and the divine will to be
is to make the other free
to grow
to be more
than he or she was before.

Him

I hate him / I love him
I despise him / I cherish him
I deplore him / I idolize him
I criticize him / I admire him
I push him out into the world / I nurture him
I show no mercy to him / I sympathize with him
I tear him down / I build him up
I laugh at him / I laugh with him
I deride his looks / I compliment his appearance
I refuse to listen to him / I accept his comments
I nag him / I am patient with him
I ignore his foolish chatter / I hang on to his every word
I douse his dreams / I encourage his ideas
I bind him closely / I give him freedom to roam
I let him suffer alone / I nurse his wounds
I let him take care of himself / I pander to his every whim
I let him live a day at a time / I plan his future for a lifetime
I don't consider his desires / I put his desires before my own
I don't worry about his taste / I cook his favorite dishes
I don't go near his truck / I wash his truck
I mourn him / I celebrate him.
Such is marriage.
Such is love.

I Thought I Heard Our Hearts

Windy days and streetlight nights —
radios, deejays, Gene's Pig and Chick,
cherry cokes, the question all the way
hamburgers except onions
cars and jobs which were not careers.
Life was night. Life was day.
Life was used up every day.

A shot rang out somewhere.
We heard it all the way down South.
And we heard it echo again and again
and we — some of us — cried,
but some laughed,
and then cried.
Another shot and then another — we asked ourselves,
"Who is our brother?"
"Lord?"
"Who is next?"
            "Who are we?"
        "Who am I?"
You offered a peach, and I said, "Peel it, please."
You did.
I heard our hearts shake hands.

The wind stopped and
the world of woes and wars and
Vietnam became the tissue
we blew our noses on
for babies, babbles, and bottles became our world.
Sunshine shone on playgrounds
and then aisles in churches.

Bells and bells and bells
and rings and rings and rings
and days honed to hours,
diced up, sliced up
into hours.
Practices/lessons/games/meetings
diced up, sliced up
filled up minutes
blocks of seven
lines of nine
bells, rings, diced up, sliced up
blocks of time.

Then quickly slowly, it was over.
A door opens down the hall
but the closet is empty —
no bells, no rings of the telephone.
I notice the cupcake pan is rusty
and can be tossed aside.

Who are we now?
And then a breeze being thing remembered —
gently, gently, gently —
A peach? Would you care for one?
A faint breeze remembered.

I thought I heard
our hearts shake hands —
again.

WAITING

Here I am
scrubbed, scented, sprayed, polished, brushed
waiting for the man I married, waiting, and waiting, and
waiting
for the man I love
the symphony, so familiar, earmarked waiting
is playing in my head
and the children already neatly tucked into their beds
and I am waiting for the phone to ring
will it be a message there's been an accident
will it be don't wait up, I am working late
is he just now turning off his desk light
is he humming to himself
waiting
for the key to turn in the door
for the smile or the frown that will greet me
waiting, waiting, and waiting, and
waiting
and the symphony plays on
when will he be coming home
and when he does,
if he does,
what will I say — how was your day
I will smile and kiss his lips and pretend
I really wasn't waiting at all
just as always
waiting.

Wear and Tear

Sometimes the one we love is like
our favorite suit of clothes
no matter the occasion

The same old suit just goes
it may have lost some eye appeal
Sometimes the one we love is like

but it fits just right
and, of course, we like its feel
no matter the occasion

It is not too loose and it is not too tight
it's true it looks worn out and faded in places
Sometimes the one we love is like

but you can't put your faith
in looks and faces
no matter the occasion

there's many a mile left in the wear and tear
of that old suit of clothes and in my honey dear
Sometimes the one we love is like
no matter the occasion.

From Her

I look at you and smile.
Do you often see me
sitting smiling like a Mona Lisa
or more recklessly
and dangerously
the smile more blatant
the faraway look gaudier?
I am a mother,
a grandmother.
I smile because she is a woman now.
A beautiful woman
little girl days are memories to her now
as well as to me.
A beauty serene, graceful, regal,
elegant, queenly,
not showy seeming. She is.
She is a woman now.
There is a mystery there
that my mind is trying to solve.
By her side is her son.
He is a young man, respected and admired.
Therein is a maze.
And I am a wife.
Therein I smile.
I look at the beard and the sprinkling of hair, colorless
yet you are stronger now with deeper hues of richest color
than before.
The twine that began a fragile thread
is now a life rope knotted by countless
inseverable kinks and bows that serves
to make it strong.
And so I smile.

FROM HIM

My wife told me I am looking old.
The stylist charged me twenty bucks
to cut this little bit of hair.
One more burden I gotta bear.

They came to appraise my house
and raised the taxes.
They must think I'm a millionaire.
One more burden I gotta bear.

Our daughter came home
and said her marriage was over.
Where is he — gone and she don't care.
One more burden I gotta bear.

My wife's brother came yesterday.
He came for a visit
but will stay a year.
One more burden I gotta bear.

My doctor took one look
and said, "Not much hope.
There's just too much wear and tear."
One more burden I gotta bear.

My coon dog died the other night
the loser in a dirt-rolling fight.
I can't live without that dog being near —
some things a man just cannot bear.

When I Walked the Aisle to You

Twenty years ago
the compass of my heart
was what I trusted
when I walked the aisle to you
for it indeed had been faith
that led me to you.
Both became the byword —
no more *yours* or *mine*.
We learned weather
made no difference —
a greater force held us together
than either held alone.
Harsh sun or beating rain
both could be our gain
for when we held hands
we were sustained.
Together we learned
that the monster we saw
when looking out the window
really had no foundation
for it was only a reflection —
a tear that needed mending
a fear that needed confronting
a hurt that needed soothing
a cloud that needed direction.
One wiser than the two of us —
the greater force was He
reminded us quite often
we must bend the knee
for when troubles had us looking up
we felt no misery.
The challenge of that moment

was to place our trust in He
who was and is
and forevermore will be.

To My Spouse When I Was Ill

The pink crepe myrtle near the drive
the dogwoods and camellias
the azaleas and the roses in their beds
are there because of me,
and if I should leave,
they'll still be here —
a part of me growing near.

When you are lonely for my face,
and the memories begin to wane,
you have only to see them growing
to think of me again.

More beauteous and better far,
the part of me that's part of you, are
our daughters, fairer than the trees and roses
that wait the morning dew
and our son the grandest warrior
I could have given you.

If by God's design I should leave,
as they grow to maturity
on them you can cleave
for what is left behind growing near your door
will be a trace of all that God
created for us before.

Need Her

If you fall in love,
need her.
If you get married,
need her.
Need her.
Need her.
Need her breath for your lungs.
Need her hair on your pillow
even if it changes color
and finally has no color or
is not there at all.
Need her.
Need her words before the rest
to fall on your ears
and to hear, really hear,
and love the best.

My Wish

I wish
I loved a man
who
had never loved
before me
that
I
would be
his
only
memory

Woman Growing

I almost forgot his birthday.
I don't remember if I kissed him
goodbye before we drove away to work
in separate cars.
Did I tell him I'd be late?
I'll email later — I need to remind him anyway
it's time for him to have an oil change and
antifreeze put in his truck.
Now, how can I remember to remember
his birthday?

Remember

"Do you remember me?"
asked the moon.
"No," I lied
as I caressed the ring worn thin on my finger.
"Did the sun dazzle you for long?"
Magic moon.
You made me bloom and
it was good in June
but all too soon —
all too soon it is November
what is left is to remember
the burning fire before the embers
of the sizzling sun.
Come back to me, magic moon,
sprinkle silver on this room
in the quietness of my gloom.

Losing My Size

Today as I walked out of the churchyard,
someone said to me,
"Gee, I never realized you were so small."
"It's simple," I replied, "I wasn't until today.
It was he who always made me tall."
I was taller
when I was
with him
than I could
ever be
alone.

POEMS ABOUT CHILDREN

I Have Wasted Days

I have wasted days, by choice,
pointing out the puzzle pieces and how they fit together
countless hours capturing images to gaze upon later
walking fingers entwined naming the leaves and birds and clouds
to children whose eyes and ears absorb each and every word
when I could have held a 9 to 5
I chose to be a 24/7
school, practices, games, lessons,
recitals, shows, parties, awards
"Why do you waste your days?" some asked.
I have wasted days by choice.
When I could have worked a routine maze,
I chose the complicated new ground of wasting days
memorizing children's laughter
that bounced around the walls and halls.
Watching children building bridges they would later climb
to find us and each other on the other side —
children, who in night's dreams look a lot like mine.
I have wasted days, by choice, and nights,
with paper in hand, helping them to pen
young passions on thin blue lines and pausing to smile.

Muffled by linens, crisp and clean,
except for bodies' excesses of love
voices breathing, echoing love words with laughter,
"We'll wake the kids."
I have wasted days, by choice,
on the trophies of our love.

FATHER AND SON

A mystery he noticed
and hung his head low.
"Into a great man I thought he would grow —
a doctor, a preacher, a scientist perhaps
but time and nature both have lapsed
and my hopes have been dashed for as
I look at him now all that I see
is that he has turned out exactly like me."
The mother heard the words
for he had breathed them aloud.
"And for that same reason
you should be proud.
No greater tribute he could give to you
than to be of the same caliber as you
and to live among men as faithful and true.
His mettle, like metal, through and through
is the strongest steel and of a beauteous hue.
A purer gold you will not behold
than the character of both are of the same mold.
Loving, hardworking, honest, sincere
he gives all of himself to God
to whom he holds dear."

Where Did All the Years Go

Where did all the years go
since we expected you
and how many days since
and we two became we three?
While your birthday was a dream day
far away in May
we cheerfully placed toys beneath the tree for you to play.
A sky-colored musical ball with a dancing horse inside
waited months for you to arrive.
All the riding horses, the toys and Sparkleberry Lane
are golden memories that forever will remain.

A Rising Star

Bumpy thumb
Hanging brothers
Bird in hand
         … Don't squeeze the bow.
Feet in position
Stand up tall
Under the chin
         … Don't let it fall.
         Elbow forward
Up on the shoulder
Keep it parallel
Rock before the *A*.

Twinkle, twinkle, Little Star
         … what a master violinist you are
you are.

Song to Marcia

Poets will write of you
Songs will be sung of you
Heaven will bless your name
Our Marcia Laine
Angels fashioned you with care
Angels watch over you here
Angels gave you your name
Our Marcia Laine
Angels guard you night and day
They protect you lest you stray
The sun shines when it rains
For our Marcia Laine
She turns roses into gold
She makes memories sweet and bold
Beauty abounds wherever she walks
Beauty breathes when she talks
Nature envies the fame
Of our Marcia Laine.
Our Marcia Laine.

My Children

Sometimes I call
but they don't come
their little feet
take them away —
there is so much
for them to touch
to pat
to squeeze
to taste
to smell
to see.
They don't stray far
till they return
when they hear my call today
but tomorrow when I call
the path of their adventures
may have taken them far away.

The DUI

The costliness of a DUI and 85 miles per hour
just four beers, not more
the sorrow
the cost
the tarnish
the lost
four beers with buddies in a bar
but passed in the solitude of a jail cell
put words on papers
took months and years to alter
put a crevice in a mother's heart
put a chasm in a father's trust.
Could be worse, that's true —
there could be a quicker death.

Mothers Make a Difference

Once my arms were strong, not flabby
when I held you as a baby

Once my nights were vigils kept
watching over the crib right steady

Days were filled and focused on baby
who wouldn't stop growing till a lady

Now I wonder where the days went
how they flew and how well spent

Did I fill your head with vanity
or prepare you for eternity?

Lost Children

A weed
stepped on or over
unfertilized in barren soil
from seed to seed
underdeveloped flowers
amass unsightly chaos
devoid of uniformity.

When each could be an heir
could lay claim
hold a right to a priestly robe
to a royal life.
If only they knew
they could choose Him —
the one who makes them His own
and puts them in the Royal Garden
tended by the King Himself.

Cain's Children

Poor Cain's children, chided,
wandering, wandering
seeking a nation to welcome them.

Poor Cain's offspring, often
misunderstood, searching
for answers, hidden with unsolvable sorrows.

Poor Cain's family, famous
for failure, never sure
but always
never.

My Mother

I think of my own little mother
and the wonder she saw in life
how she made a simple story
capture my mind with strange delight
how she did everything without complaining
from early morning to late at night
knowing tomorrow she'd have it all to do again
and always with love, laughter, and singing
with lots of hugging and kissing.
Building dreams and confidence in our heads
that one day we would be a parent too
and know exactly what to do.
But now somedays the job just gets too big
and I'll cry or fuss or forget to sing.
Then, out of the blue, it seems to me
I'll think of Mama and hear her say
It's alright. Everything will be okay.

The Path

I'm making
a path some ways wide and
some ways
narrow
for you and yours
and I hope
that you will do
so too
for
all
the
ones
who
will
come
after
you
for
four decades
almost five
I see
behind me
the way
ahead
winds
and wanes
with
wonder
but a certain
certainty.

Tribute to Frankie

Tell me one more time
if you don't mind
how do we know each other
Tell me if you will
for I may forget again
Did you say you are my daughter
which one
or is there another
Tell me if you will
for I may forget again
Oh, that is my mother
I remember her so well
and that is my dear daddy!
This photo rings a bell.
But tell me one more time
if you don't mind
how do we know each other
Tell me if you will
for I may forget again
Did you say I used to be a teacher
Did I teach you
or did we teach together
Tell me your name once more
Tell me if you will
for 1 may forget again
I'm only here for a little while
soon I'll be going home
I can't seem to find my way at present
now that I'm alone
Thank you for coming to see me
It is really good to see you
But tell me one more time

if you don't mind
how we know each other
Tell me if you will
for I'll forget again.

Helicopter

How is it that you go
up and down
like a giant mosquito hawk?
Is that why
Black Hawk is the name of a chopper?
Are you a chopper because your blades
chop-chop-chop
the air with that same sound?
Is it easier to fly a big fly
than a gigantic jet?
With your easy access door
do you feel secure
with your feet of skis?
Do you rest easier on water or a land sliver?
Which one makes your liver quiver?

The Dog that Chased Its Tail

Each day the bus route
took us by the yard of
the dog that chased its tail.
He never let us down —
he was there each day
it was sad the way
he had created
a circular track
deeper and deeper
in the clay
was this his play
chasing his tail but
never catching it.

Your Visit

You came to call that wintry day
on strangers in a lonely town —
I remember well your dress was blue,
but your eyes were brown.
The smile you wore was summer.

I don't remember what you said
to Dad or Mom or me
but through the years, time after time,
your summer smile I see.
It was cold but you were summer.

Each time we had to move away
to a different lonely town
I always looked and hoped for you
and your eyes of brown
and the scent of summer.

Parents, Listen, Please

Give up excess drinking.
Give up drugs for fun.
Believe in yourself;
believe in God.
Save your children
by saving yourself.
Believe in yourself;
believe in God.
Your children are wandering
in the darkness.
They need you
to show them the way.
To be a role model
you must be strong
by believing in yourself
and believing in God.
Believe you can make it
without drinking and drugs.
Lead them out of the darkness
by following God.
Show them you care about yourself
about them
about God.
God gave them to you
for you to care for them.
Show them that you love them
by doing what is best for them.
Believe in yourself
believe in God.
Parents, listen to me, you can do it.
Believe in yourself,
be strong, believe in God.

Parents, keep telling yourself,
"I know I can do it!
With God's help I can make it!"
God will help you
save yourself and
save your children.

Daughter's Wedding

Four months till daughter's wedding
the roar is in my ears
while night is here, rest is ebbing
sleep is the wave rushing in and snatched back
before it reaches the shore
though spring is not official
mid-summer is my goal
the swift quick days in between have much too much to hold
the altar decorations
the cakes the punch the flowers
the dresses rice bags — but birdseed
the photographs the video
the music and the singers
the bridesmaids' dresses the money
the dress that I will wear
the guest list
the postage stamps "We must use the Love stamp, please!"
invitations out
the food the meats
the tablecloths
the vegetables the dips
the candles centerpieces
ferns
palms (mine are already wet)
will spring days be long enough
to do all we have to do
and do it perfectly and
not forget a single thing or two
the house —
will they get the house
is the realtor on the ball
Lord they don't even have a stove

or refrigerator
I'll think about this later
for now the thief, the wedding,
robs me of my rest
while, he, the father of the bride
lies there, snoring at his best
sleep now, sweetheart, enjoy your peace
your time is yet ahead
when bills begin to come like ocean spray
you'll toss upon the sea of matrimony past
yes, you'll toss upon this bed.

Between Ages

For a while last night
I ate my fingernails down —
It was not for fear of being alone —
I wasn't —
for *he* was there
ten pounds of humanity with a bit of hair
How I wished I could have been two people
I was somewhere
in between
mother and child
between
the ubiquitous fears
for mother's maladies and mortality
and
ubiquitous smiles and charms of this child
who inflates my heart until I think
others must notice it rise and fall
My mother, far away, babbling in her bed
My heart was heavy I could not be there
to hold her hand
What if God calls her away tonight?
I was sitting with my first grandchild, a blessed July delight.
My fears were sharp
I bit my nails in worry
for I was somewhere in between
Until
he looked at me
and laughed
communicating in language indescribable
he knew I comprehended
his four-week-old smile put my fears aside.
May it be like this

somewhere in the future
when I waste away
in a hospital bed
vacated by my mother —
when I babble at this baby
and he then a man
will comprehend
and cause all my fears subside.

Grandma's Rocking Chair

Sometimes people think she's a hundred and three
'cause she puts her rocking chair up in a tree
and won't come down for no one but me.

I go to the tree and look up and say
"Grandma, will you come down to play today?"
She hops right up from that rocking chair
and walks to the end of the limb over there.
She slides down that invincible rope
that nobody notices but Grandma and me.
Then she's down on the ground to play with me.

I know Grandma's age is the same age as mine.
We run and play and have a fun time.
She takes off her shoes and says,
"Wow — that feels fine"
but she doesn't care that I leave on mine.

She says, "Now that I'm old, I don't have to wear shoes.
Now is the time to do what *I choose*
and I choose *not* to wear shoes today.
I'll let my toesies out to play, play, play."

She likes to play with each of my toys
and told me, "When I was a kid,
this toy was only for boys.
Girls could play with dolls and such,
but I wanted to play with trains and trucks."

She jumps on my scooter and
flies down the street —
faster than lightning —

she's only a streak.
Someone says, "What in the devil was that?"
And someone else answers, "Just that old bat
who keeps her rocker up in a tree
trying to act like a kid on a spree."

Grandma's moving too fast to hear,
but if she did, she still wouldn't care.
She'd say, "Be careful when you judge others
for the things they do.
Judging causes others to judge you.

"I should be *I*, and you should be *you*.
You see, there's plenty of planet
for each boy and each girl
to have a safe circle in this big world.
It's a big enough place for every *he* and *she*
to fly down the street on a scooter, being free,
or to rock, if you like, in the top of a tree."

A Mama's Song

The cell phone —
cradled — in her palms —
call to home
fingers paying alms
fingers entwined
Mama singing psalms
here is mine
here is the church
be kind
here is the steeple
heart in a lurch
open the doors
on its perch
here are the people
like a sequel
God, are You in for chores
is my world to topple
remember he is one of Yours
will it ring
just a K would mean so much
would make me sing
it would be a touch
I'm alive
or such
I can drive
I'm not on IVs
yes, I still survive
God, let it ring, please
One more time
Please

POEMS ABOUT LIFE, NATURE, AND DEATH

Short Visits

I sat resting a moment
when they passed
the tall beautiful pair
white in white and fair.
They marched through the door
that slid open for them
and then to another open door
and up they went.
Too soon they marched past again
in the opposite direction —
duty done
and on their way.
Often as I come
to stand or sit or pray beside a bed,
I think of them —
who quickly came that day,
the tall beautiful pair
white in white and fair
who will never know that someone would see
and put them in a poem because of their brevity.
I wonder
when life demands more time
and chunks of it are chiseled off beside sick beds
I wonder
who was waiting up the stair that day
and what of more importance took the pair away?
Where are they now
the sick one and the pair
the tall beautiful pair
white in white and fair?

SMALL-TOWN BOY DONE GOOD

He's just a small-town boy done good.
He's done better than anyone thought he could.
He followed God's call and gave it his all.
He never meant to run ahead of the rest,
but he's turned out to be one of the best.

He was born with a dream in his head
and by God he was easily led.
In his heart he had his own song
and held on to his dream all along.

He must have seen the invisible track
but didn't forget his way back.
From the Opry to records and Bill Gaither too
he shared the story of Jesus so true.

He still holds to ideals of his youth —
love of country and God and the truth.
Deep inside he's the same —
he knows life's more than a game.

He's just a small-town boy done good.
just look at what he's done.
For himself he made a good name
and is honoring God with his fame.

Frumpy Frog

You'd best respect the earthworm
and the frumpy frog
for if either goes
man will not be long.
Goodness sakes! Oh, me!
And don't forget the honeybee.

Soft Snow

Soft snow,
oh, how the south sun thaws you!
Though we celebrate you,
we cannot contain you.
Though we photograph your beauty
and excuse your bigotry,
you will not linger.
You tease and test us senseless
for our denseness
in our defenselessness.
We are forever in anticipation.
Soft snow, soft snow
oh, how the south sun thaws you!

School Is a Place for Remembering

School is a place for remembering —
a place for learning how to remember
rules for games and
hopefully, God's rules and truths for the game of life
universal music measures and facts and figures of math and science
and someone's account of someone's history.

School is a place for remembering —
the students
they come and go, they come and go
some write — today they text —
their names on our memory
some of our names get printed on some of theirs.

School is a place for remembering —
but sometimes, for some minds,
for students and teachers and coaches,
and counselors, and principals and secretaries and librarians
and bus drivers and cafeteria workers and security officers
and substitute teachers and school nurses and volunteers,
and any others who pass through its gears
sometimes the rules and truths and facts and figures
become blurred or faded or twisted
and what remains is
an essence
a nuance
a connotation
a whiff
a feeling
a realization
a partial memory we nurture.

Finally, school is a place for remembering that —
the wheels on the bus go round and round and
the wheels on the school go round and round and
the people in the bus go up and down and
the people in the schools go up and down
all the way from the past to the future.

The Lies They Tell

Someone else's mirror —
like someone else's camera —
they lie —
especially those mall mirrors —
in the stalls in the shops
where you try on clothes —
they lie.
I tell you —
look at the image
in your head
juxtaposed to the store mirror —
whoever designed that mirror was twisted
and those cameras are worse —
they capture the lie —
like a billboard or banner in the sky
blaring out to others —
Look how old —
Look at that fat —
See the sagging here and there —
Oh, I wonder,
whose body did they borrow
and how did they do away with mine?

Going Overboard

Why, oh why, can't there be
balance in my life
harmony, real symmetry
even keel
actually not too uneven
on a scale
not a bell curve with a mean
not a line down the middle
with two opposite sides
even parallels
but all mixed up like a yogurt maker does
yogurt in a pound cake with consistent
textures tastes
like green tea
that is not distant extremes
one minute sweet, next minute sour?
Why can't my life be like that?
Just give me a hint
not even
a full-fledged ounce of anything
and I go crazy hyperbolizing
blowing an iota far out of proportion —
it's a Family Dollar Store balloon one second
and a balloon sailing across the sky the next —
you know the kind with baskets and people in them
hot air balloons
yes — that's it exactly.
Just give me a hint of anything with innuendos of success
for instance and the very next minute
there's old me up in the blue sky
riding in that hot air balloon
nothing but hot air

no reason for it
none at all
no actual foundation
just plain old hot air exaggerations
going overboard upward
that's a good description of me.
Just when I think there's an idea
just an idea, mind you,
old me goes and grows it in
one gulp of breath into a
monstrosity of false reality
and by then the dream of
ever achieving an even keel life is
blown to smithereens.
Why did I ever imagine I could hit the sky
with success
or fulfill or complete a book?
Why would I think that
first a seed then poof — up I go
growing a sycamore or an old oak
and placing Christmas ornaments all around the branches —
See how absurd the idea
going upward overboard
Christmas lights on a sycamore?

If I Don't Come Back

If I don't come back
how will you remember me
by what you see
in how I look
the clothes I wear
the way I fix my hair
whether or not
I've shaved my legs and
whether or not
I'm wearing socks
Would you remember me
by what I do in hours off and on
how I try
to slip in a room
unnoticed
and voice an opinion quietly
not to upset the status quo
except in matters
that matter to someone
other than mere me
or will it be that I only thought of me
all the time it was me
perhaps that is why I ask this question
How will you remember me?
When you no longer see me
what is the decree?
It was just a few years
just a few friends
just a few smiles
just a few tears
just a few miles
just a few of you

just a few of me —
So I ask again what will it be?
When we are catapulted eons away
into a future destination —
what of me will you remember?

THE BROOK

I stole time
to sit today
I stole space
beside a brook away
a paradise
swift clear waters
flowing over ghostly stones
searching for identity
searched for eternity
a stranger stared back at me
from the cold, too cold, waters
from the swift, too swift, waters
flowing
flowing
flowing
flowing
pass
and said to me
There's time
Reach out —
grasp!
Do not fear the cold
Be bold!

The Flight of the Profound

My professional thoughts have disappeared
which earlier today I felt the direst need to record
as I brushed my teeth —
they came like ladybug beetles
which have invaded our house of late
write me down
my plethora of thought
my mania of mental activity
begged
but now, hours later,
I can only hear Romeo say,
"Peace, Mercutio, you speak of nothing."

Passing Death

I pass death a thousand times a day
each time
a hand invisible
extends to shield me
blocking
greedy death away
Mighty fingers bold
hold me
warning scorning
death
so death slinks back
and leaves me free to walk another mile.
The invisible hand must know a secret.
Therein, I smile.

Straightening Up

The time had come
I was of the age
to prioritize
focus on the necessary
bite the bullet as they say.
Made the list and vowed to do it
straighten up my life
get rid of all that brings me harm
or waste my quickly evaporating time.
Took the boxed games and puzzles
with the missing pieces
and half-read tomes
to Salvation Army
no more alcohol — all booze has to go
to cigarettes — an emphatic no
no more sugar, red meats, fats,
scratched chocolate from my list
limit time on TV, cell phone, and shopping
sleep less but better
I put chocolate on the list?
exercise, exercise, exercise
read the Bible, pray
quality time with friends
I put chocolate on the list?
Did I think I could?
Did I think at all?
I try to hone myself to the bone,
and be the best I can
but chocolate cannot be gone
chocolate makes the man.
To addictions I say nevermore
but leave ajar the door
for chocolate.

We Country Sisters

Corn is growing there
where once was a floor.
Furrows now borrow the path
which once led to our door.
On the ground where the house
in which we were born
now stands a field of tall swaying corn.
The frame of the little house
were chinaberry trees
their umbrella branches loaded
with sweet peas —
we little barefoot girls
with dirty elbows and skint knees.
The smell of ham and coffee
in evening filled the air
the supper call was
Daddy's truck we'd hear.
Daddy sharpened neighbors' saws
and Mama milked the cows
and cooked and washed the clothes
a mile of them on the line it seemed
two worlds in one, ours and theirs,
reality versus dreams.

Daddy went first to a new home
and Mama followed near.
The used-up old house
a photograph we hold dear.
The chinaberry trees
are almost a forgotten memory
as if they were never there.
The aroma of brewing coffee

no longer fills the air.
But tall stalks sway majestically
without a single care
and wave hello again and again
to we girls of yesteryear.

Twentieth Century

There was a time I had some dreams,
shining stars in a lucid black night sky
but that was long ago
way back then, it did not seem so very far
to a sky in a galaxy in the Milky Way.
But everyone wanted a piece of me
and took all but what you now see.
Was I used up way back down the road to eternity?
Does anybody here
remember my name?
I've been here so long,
I've forgotten why I came.
I cannot recall exactly
who I was when I arrived —
Did someone move the sky?
Did anybody hear that I had died?

We Put Off Being Happy

We put off being happy
for reasons from A to Z
then we sit and wonder
when that happy time will be —
an apathetic husband
a brother deep in sin
a chronic case of something
a daughter's shady friend
envy of a neighbor
finances uncontrolled
gray hairs found this morning
the house is getting old
in-laws, they're a bother
jealousy galore
kitchen needs remodeling
love's gone out the door
medical bills and mortgages
nosy neighbors down the street
obligations, obesity
payments we can't meet
quick to judge another's faults
too rash to show compassion
something someone said one day
teachers, tempers, taxes
urban life gets me down
we need a long vacation
weather hasn't been too good
x-radiation
yellow eyes stare back each day
the zodiac's to blame
we put off being happy —
oh, what a loss and shame!

To Holden

I'll tell you where the ducks go
when the winter winds blow.
I'll tell you where the ducks go
since you really want to know.
They go where you and I go
when the winter winds blow.
We hate the hiss and the howl
of the hungry, angry wind
so we bury ourselves
inside of the seed of self within.
Dormant we lie till
the seed of ourselves
in the soil of our soul
is reborn in the busy-ness of spring.

Poets and Prisoners

Travel on the life track?
Backpack?
Coming back?
Which side the track?
Going where?
I don't care.
Like a bird in the air.
On the train?
In the main?
That the kind
you mean?
Straight line.
Doing time.
Just time
any time
do you mind?
It's my time
Hey, yeah, I mind.
Rails, rails, rails
hard and cold and always
lines
apart, separating,
separate.
They must cross to multiply
or add,
but half a line
takes away.
There must be a house to
go to,
but half a line
takes away.
Go away

lines
and rails
and let a man be free.
Two kinds.
Some will bring us joys untold
while others bring us pain.
Some will test our souls
while others give it back again.
We too are to them the same
that we greet
in deeds done to brothers
that we chance to meet.
Some in fancy finery will see us
simple and shake their heads
and sigh.
They will breathe an insult and
quickly pass us by.
Some will use us for their pastime
abuse our sincere self.
When we serve their need no longer,
they will set us on a shelf.
Others, out of envy, will ignore
our earnestness
gossip, spite, and whisper,
even hiss at our success.
Then there is another brother
who drew interest on our honor
who plucked away a passing smile
we gave them one fine hour.
Also there is a child
who saw a kindness in our eyes
and in a spoken word we said,

saw a Savior who for us had died.
What is the person others see
when the rails crisscross pass me?
Do they see God's hand at work?
Do they see a Christlike man?
Do they see sincerity?
Do they see a brother?
Do they see a loving father?
A model of a mother?
Are you the person you would like to meet
on the Rails-of-Life Street?

Riches

As I wore away
at wishing wealth
I saw the thing
over there
with tiny wings
that broke through
and grew
then the thing
flew away.
Riches I had
in my hand
cold and hard
while over there
the beauty was warm
alive
then gone.

Roll on Wheels

The mind is spinning the wheels.
The body idles.
The battery is going dead.
Get up from your bed.
Get your mind in gear.
Sit up.
Dare to raise your head up
from your desk and give
the gas to your dreams.
Step into the driver's seat.
Follow the road map.
Keep your eyes up ahead.
Too soon the ride is over.
You lose time by delay.
Turn the key and get going.
The flag is down —
Be on your way!

It's a New Day

His wool was gray
and his mound of a body was bent over
on the side of the road
fishing in a ditch.
I wanted to stop
to ask
"Why a ditch?
Are there no ponds nearby?
Are you too old, too feeble
to walk to a pond
or do you have no one —
no one to help you get to
deeper, wider water?
The day is new —
are you living a memory
when a boy
you fished in a ditch
and perhaps made a meal?
But today is new,
Old Man,
especially for you."

THE HOME

As they are
so we will be
folded flobs
of humanity
vacant visions
in nodding
snow-covered
mountain peaks
lids blinking back
unsayable
terrible passions
or is it
passionate terrors?

Winding Time

Each Sunday morning
he would bend down
to take up the key
to open the door
to wind the clock —
the grandfather clock
that stood in the corner
of the most elegant room
in the house
for by late Saturday night
there was hardly a tick
hardly a swing of the pendulum
and if you looked deeply into the heart of the clock
you'd wonder if another second could pass.
Winding the clock on Sunday morning
as he has done year after year
was crucial
for then
he could
stand up
and face time
unafraid.

Plastic Bags in Roadside Trees

vacation
scenic route
sightseers
credit cards
plastic bags
plastic bags in roadside trees
in the tops and limbs and between
Paper? Plastic?
Plastic dis-decorates the trees.
Paper, on the other hand,
is the gift
trees give to man.

Winter Makes a False Return

Why does the winter chill return
jilting spring
the perishing pear blossoms
pallor victims of the impious snow
bruised by the brutal soft snow
that which would have grown
to ripen and sweeten the world
will now never be
the early promises are gone you see
but there will be many more
and my heart will be excited
and my taste buds be delighted
when winter is gone for good
and pears will hang on the limbs
as they should
until ripened and eaten —
oh! so good!

SEA AT NIGHT

Did you ever see
the sea at night
from ten floors high
beneath a moon
reflecting itself off the
sliding sheets of the sea
arriving in timely order one after another
on the scalloped shore?
Like the moon,
being much higher
with a scope much wider
and keener the eye
from His spot in the sky,
surely God must delight
in the sight
of the sea
at night.

Forsythia

When the golden forsythia brightens up the snow,
I make my plans to propagate even more —
a hedge of them —
thousands of them —
around the perimeter of the entire place.
Only one I brought from Mama's yard
that day —
the day after they took her
and her worldly things away.
All you must do to grow them is to extend the sprig
for it takes root in any soil and bursts forth so big —
like her —
with arms outstretched to all she ever knew —
reaching out and giving
was all she knew to do.
When winter should be ending
but remains fickle, cold,
I'll have those arms around me
to make me warm and bold.
Forsythia breaks out silently
to bid the snow goodbye
unafraid, in gold, helps us remember why
our hearts fill at new beginnings
with the ability to cope
for within the flower there is ever hope —
exactly what we long
for in our darkest hour.
Before the other flowers even consider showing up —
except perhaps the jolly jonquil,
the oxymoronic stalwart of fragility,
who loves to shout, "It's over! It's finally over."
When it seems nonexistent,
gold and spring and Mama
are but a missed breath away.

GASTON WATER MAN

He's known by all in these parts
when he comes down the street.
The silver haired man, a quick smile sweet,
that kids come to see him and grab his hand.
He's known by one and all as Papa Pound
or the Gaston Water Man.
People wave when they see the plumber's white van
for they know they will be blessed by seeing
the Gaston Water Man.
He can fix that leak. Yes, he can!
Mister, you must be a stranger in this here land
if you don't know Papa Pound aka
the Gaston Water Man.

Life

In my mother's womb
I heard the sound of the sea
It was the sunrise
that greeted my eyes
The moment her body
set me free
The taste in my mouth
was the salt of the sea
and sand was my cradle
Fine sand, hard sand
Fine sand, soft sand
Fine sand, hard sand
Fine sand, soft sand
My hair swayed in the wind
like the sea oats
all day till the evening
when the steel of the sea
met the gray of the sky
Fine sand, hard sand
Fine sand, soft sand
Fine sand, hard sand
Fine sand, soft sand
but the sound of the sea
was the same.

LIFE THROUGH SOMEONE ELSE'S EYES

Life blossoms and
shows us the flower we are
the poetry of life that's driven in our DNA
before our life began
to spring forth anew as time goes on
in each and every man.
Life is too wonderful
and passes too quickly
not to lengthen your days
by laughing at yourself
once in a while.
The weight of the world's worry
disappears as you look at yourself
through someone else's eyes
and then realize
they are doing the same.

When You Are Grown

When you are grown
and home is gone
and you're supposed to be in control
of all emotions, the seat of tranquility,
for those who look to you
to see an example of maturity.
Inside your heart is a homesick child,
who would like nothing more
than to be like the broomstick waiting behind the door,
for Mama's hands to hold you close once more.
But that home is not there anymore.
And the little girl inside
longs to hear her daddy say,
"We've been looking for you, Sugar,
all this livelong day."
Thoughts of going home
only bring the tears
for now you are grown up
and you have been for years.
You have grandkids who never saw your mom and dad
and never considered the playground you once had.

Two Different Kinds

One girl wouldn't dream of going out
with curlers in her hair —
the decision of her day
was what and what not to wear.

The other, on the other hand,
looked pieced and thrown together
and went about bareheaded
in rain or sunny weather.

While one was prim and pretty
as a picture anytime
the other looked an error
of the proper kind.

Sisters they were and sisters they are
and you best know and see
speak ill of either one
and you'll pay the penalty.

NEIGHBORS

Who is a neighbor?
I'll tell you what I know.
I see two trees
a pine and dogwood
and side by side they grow.
One needs the sun,
one needs the shade —
they're neighbors.
I see the cows
lingering along the path
and the horses
eating the same grass —
they're neighbors.
I see the cardinal and the jay
who share the bath and tray
in their own way —
they're neighbors.
In the quietness of my day,
I know that you are there
and I mention you in prayer.
In all that you do
I know you say my name too —
we're neighbors.

Planting the Future

Her snowy white head
uncovered, unbound
she's out of her wheelchair
hands and knees on the ground

My frail weak neighbor
with her little great-grand
and a basket of bulbs
and a grandiose plan

In the midst of October weather
under a topaz sky,
"She won't live till spring
to see them bloom," I sigh.

Turning I continued to complete
the same jobs I do every day
of the week, every week
every day in the very same way.

The thought came to me
that she might want more
from life than I and others like me
who are tied to their chores.

For she sees
into the eyes of tomorrow
where golden blooms wave
with no shadow of sorrow.

Can we in twelve hours of our day fulfill
as much as the planting of daffodils?

GRACE IS THE CREAM

Mama would milk the cow every evening
and pour the milk in a two-quart bowl
and set it in the refrigerator.
A scientific phenomenon occurred overnight —
the rich delicious cream in the milk
that we could not see with our naked eye
rose to the top.
In relationships it is often hard to tell
who is a friend and who is a foe
who will harm you as you go.
If someone hurts you —
and some will —
you must love them still.
You cannot control their actions —
only how you opt
and remember always —
cream rises to the top.

A Daylily in Heaven

I know heaven
along with the gates of pearl
is going to have all those precious stones —
streets of gold —
walls of jasper, emerald, sapphire, diamond, and all.
Stones are beautiful to look at,
but stones don't have fragrance
and are hard to the touch —
Now a daylily —
yes, a daylily, Lord,
if a choice I'm given
would be perfect for your heaven.

Choose Love

When someone ignores you,
choose to love.
When someone speaks ill of you,
choose to love.
When someone cheats you,
choose to love.
When someone despises you,
choose to love.
When someone attacks you,
choose to love.
You *always* have a choice —
choose to love.

Prejudice

People's pride's proof
ruins relationships
ends equality
judges joy
usurps divides
injures innocent inspiration
chides children's creativity
erodes opportunities for eternity.

The Hair in Our Character

It was over our salads
and the Sunday sermon rehashed
when I noticed it —
the hair protruding
from my friend's nose.
We've been friends forever
but I had never noticed
such a defect —
strange —
for we were much alike.
Stranger still
when I got home
and looked in the mirror
and saw the hair that grows
protruding from my nose.

The Casket Truth

Framed
in her casket
with her
was her
life
and her words:
See
what life did
to me.

They

They can tell you all kinds of things
usually it's stuff
that's scary and bad
but
they never have to stand up to their criticisms
they say this and
they say that
but
they never show their faces.
It would be prudent to make *they*
prove what *they* so often
disapprove.

Talk Time

I never get enough
talk time
my thoughts take longer
to put into words because there are many words
to choose from and the exact word is important
but I don't get a chance to say them precisely
because someone else butts in
to finish my thoughts
obliterate my thoughts
compromise my thoughts
or say their own contrary thoughts
fast thoughts
streamlined
fresh
my thoughts take longer
to put into words, it's true,
but I am left way back there
not finished thinking them through.

Fear

Chopin-like icicles
crackling and falling with
interruptions an army of advancing
horses
unsteeled nerves
moving toward a chasm
an abyss dismal
muted blinded eye-
opening freight train
future.

Old Drivers

Old drivers put on the brakes going downhill.
"Drats!" I slapped the steering wheel.
Just when I need to get there in a hurry,
I have to get behind some senior citizen!
Wait a minute,
I am a senior citizen and
I am always in a hurry.
My PhD class will start in ten minutes and
it will take me longer than that
to find a parking place.

How Dare You

There is still a me
though I had to learn winter
would you dare measure me
really
by what rule
would you mark the meaning of my soul
value my humanity
my faith in God and fellowman
would you hold a number stick to my character
and every decision
I have ever made
that let-another-win sense
by what scale do you weigh my worth
with words
which balance does your bias use
to choose if I am worthy
for there are many scales
and there is still a me.

Close Distance

I brushed shoulders
with a kind of happiness once
tasted fate and fame
almost shook hands
with a kind of destiny
fingertips touched
momentary intersections of
opportunity and then
the light changed.

Weekends

I like to open 'er up on Fridays
in the right lane
on I-26
and see the envy in their eyes
as I whiz by
as I whiz whiz whiz by —
School and work are over
and I am on my way
the beach is calling
I answer I am on my way!
I live weekdays for the beach
can't wait till I get there
the sand and salt
is all I want
by Monday in the left lane
I will have left it all again.

Youth

Some plunge headlong
flailing arms and wide-eyed
open thrilling
like diving off the high board
their maxims do not miss
a solitary situation.
But some with squeezed tight eyes
wish it would pass quickly
so they could be in some setting
where they will never be
they only want acceptance
and acceptable reality.

I Agree, Emily

Hope is the sound
of the minute bird
off in the distant tree,
that —
if you listen —
grows sweeter and clearer
with each calamity.

Big Busy Sky

Each opponent seemed to say
"I'm very busy. Stay out of my way."
Upon the stage each one flew
too busy to notice a director's cue
who might have said
"Slow down a bit. We are sure to have a hit."
Squirrels passing on the stage
in vertical lines from side to side
occasionally jumping and always jumpy
freezing only for a second to squish their tails
darting and dashing were the tiny wrens
scratching for the tiniest seeds and flying back again
flitting to any niche they could fit in
cardinals from shrub to shrub gently graciously
ladybugs swarmed in gossipy clouds
engaging the air with warmest brown

The lunch break is over and past
students now rush to their next class.

Road Signs and Sighs

The scarred trees live to tell the tale
the pink plastic flowers
at their unreal roots
are signatures
of silenced voices that once sang
the speeding cars on I-26 whiz by
their drivers glance
and hear only a
fragment of their songs
for the theme is
universal
a mangled canine body stiff
the once lithe and agile deer —
here and there
but no pink plastic.

The Lowly Horn

Horns are good
to have
for horns can warn
the Lincoln in the left lane
crossed the line
but just in time
the BMW blew his horn
quite a quick blare
and the Lincoln was spared despair.

The Island

An artificial naturalism drapes this island land
like the dead-looking living Spanish moss
in live oak trees
villages of yesterday
on the weekend hours visited
by professional natives
unrecognized
by this land

Atheists

I
do
believe
that some people
have become atheists
because they simply don't
want to put up Christmas trees
and
decorations!

The Eulogy

The three grandchildren in the front turned
in their unfamiliar cramped place in the pew
between the young women in black dresses
and the tall son in just-bought black suit
to see the one who had waited till last to speak.
"He was my friend,"
the standing man said, his best friend Frank,
and then the words were lost in loving remembrance
and his best friend Frank ended the way he began —
"He was my friend."

Beach at Sunrise

The shaggy beard of black reeds
washed in
are threatened by the shaving cream looking
rolling a lone reed rolling
not aligned with the sea
passes
will it succeed
it rests, supported by another
that is aligned with the mighty roar of the sea
How long will these two last?
Not long.
But longer together than alone.

Double Stitched

The family
that can laugh
at each other
shows
it is double stitched —
double stitched
at the seams.

What I Used to Be

What I used to be, I ain't.
What I used to could do, I cain't.
Needless to say, I've had my day
and that's about all I have to say.

They Hand Her the Folded Flag

Once a baby warm and snug
filled her arms with pride and love
but today they will blow a bugle
and shoot a round in the air
for the son who had danced around her heart
is no longer there.

Once he held her close to him
after vows had been exchanged
but today her arms are empty
she aches to hold him once again
but today they will blow a bugle
and shoot a round in the air
for the husband who had filled her head with dreams
is no longer there.

Once their days became ecstatic
as his presence filled the room
Daddy was like no other
to ease pain and dispel gloom
but today they will blow a bugle
and shoot a round in the air
for the daddy who had kissed their hurts away
is no longer there.

All their lives he'd been their hero
they had known it all along
that the heroes of this world
don't always look tough and strong.

I only did my duty.
I was no hero he would say
when God or country calls
there is no better way.

Courage and wisdom come when needed
from God up above
to fight evils of this world
doing right against all that's wrong.

Wisdom to choose the battle
comes from God above too.
To fight an honorable battle
a soldier must be true.

Not every soldier's battlefield
looks one and the same
most are fought in silence
compared to a chess game.

The substance of a soldier
lies in obeying the call to go
and fight the raging battles
of which others may not know.

Today each must be a hero
and duty must not lag
when after the bugle sounds
and they shoot a round
and hand her the folded flag.

If I Had Known It Would Be the Last Time

When I saw you alone on the barstool,
I slipped by without saying a word.
It was the first time I'd ever seen you
without enclosing you in a hug.
You see, I'm not really that complicated;
with me it's black or white, tried and true,
biases are my weakness
but shouldn't have applied to you.
And if I'd known it would be the last time
of ever seeing you,
I would have ignored all the gossip and innuendos,
and this is what I would do.
I would stop and hug you so tightly
holding on to those shoulders
once so strong and broad.
I'd tell you I believe in you
no matter what went wrong.
I wouldn't ask you any questions.
I wouldn't tell you any lies.
I'd forget the bygone days
and all the tears that I cried.
I'd tell you I believe in you, honey,
and I'm here for you always
and I'd stay there by your side forever
till I'd see the old you in your eyes.

POEMS ABOUT GOD

❁

Until I Was Thirty

Until I was thirty
I thought I was perfect and always right.
After that I began to know
on life's gamut I ranged on the side of imperfect
and often wrong.
It was then I began to learn to deal with acceptance —
a test for the human race.
Then I became sixty.
I need to readjust my thinking once again
my logic has been all wrong
for what had come to pass in this world has left us all undone.
In ways of eternity, we certainly are not one.
Though made by God, there's still a race to be run.
One thing sets us apart —
the matter of the heart.
Our choice is the key
in where we spend eternity.

Just When You Think

Just when you think that you have it all —
a house in the mountains, and one on the shore
life is so full
you don't need anymore
the spouse is content
the children behaving
microwave and dishwasher safe
the future is absolutely raving

Then it happens —

The bottom falls out —
the market collapses
the bank takes the houses
the spouse can't take it and
walks out the door
the kids need things you can't provide anymore
the dreams are shattered
you've lost it all —
and you aren't even sure
how it happened —
you can't recall.
Just yesterday you said
life can't get any better than this
your life was filled with joy, pure bliss
your home was completely safe and secure
and now you stand alone before the abyss.
In a moment everything is chaos
empty filled with defeat
if it were food there'd be nothing to eat

You used to go to the church and pray
sad to say, it's been many a day
and they wouldn't remember your name anyway
but maybe just maybe today is the day

you tell the kids we're going this time
they look at you as if you've lost your mind
first to greet you is that old guy Joe
are these your kids, man, way to go
they're growing up fast these days, you know
a new pastor's here he's really young
full of energetic handshakes and oozing with love
You stand in the pew thinking you're all alone —
Why did I come here when everything's gone —

Then it happens —

You feel arms wrap you in a tender embrace
You hear a faint whisper, this is called grace
I've known you forever, knit you in the womb
I'll be with you forever, even after the tomb
You can't explain what —
you can't explain how —
you can't explain why He could love you that much —
but it happened
You know HE IS
You know HE CARES
whatever comes and whatever goes
you're not alone
He's by your side
supplying more power than you've ever known
you can laugh at tomorrow
for He shares your sorrow.
But for this day, for this crystallized minute in time,
when you felt defeated, lost, and alone
just when you thought
you had nothing to live for
you find, with Him,
you have it all.

CLOSE OR LOST

"He came *so close*,"
somebody said,
"but, you know, it's true,
being *so close* will never ever do."

So close to being all-in,
God's total man,
giving all to He who paid the cost —
he came so close but still was lost.

He put off the most important
a little at a time,
saying, "Not now, not today."
Other things were on his mind.

Satan's favorite challenge
to change the course of men
is to say, "You are close enough —
you don't have to go all-in."

You Meant Heaven to Me

Some people
are always trying to tell you
that
you're nothing
but
Jesus says,
you meant
heaven to Me.

Troubled Times

In troubled times our burdens cause us
to bend or break or grow.
Leaning on a higher source
is the surest way to go.
Grasping the mighty hand of God,
we surely will not fall
for He is ever near us
to help us when we call.
It's true! Our broken hearts
can be mended and made fresh, anew
for He is always there reaching out to you.
He alone gives solace and hope to every man.
In troubled times we need Him to help us stand.
Not only troubled times
but for all the way
choose Christ as your companion
every single day!

Others' Jobs

When I try to help,
I'm all thumbs
and trip over my own two feet.
"You're in the way," they're too nice to say.
It's "Come again another day."
Why can't it be easier to fit into a team
and help the work to flow
instead of messing up and causing it to slow?
Maybe it's someone else's job I am trying to do.
Maybe God is saying, "Do the work I have *for you*."

Prayer Bias

Praying
over someone's
needs
never eliminates
or takes precedence over
celebrating with thankfulness
his blessings
from the One
who made them possible.

The Me Inside

The me inside
sometimes comes out
like a waterspout
and spews the me
I don't want others to see
all over the image
I am trying to be.

Often in times
of hurry
or worry
I cannot control or keep it in —
the me —
that resides within.

The me —
the good me
the nice me
the righteous me —
the me others could admire
is now a tarnished image
that stinks like filthy mire.

While others think
that hypocrite,
Jesus says of my regret
you are a work in progress
you are not finished yet.

CHRISTIAN GEEKS' PRAYER

Log on to my heart, Lord.
Browse my folders and my files
and delete the files that are
merely taking up space
and lowering my capacity to serve You.

Delete these files, Father;
don't even send them to the
recycle bin
if they are alien to Your will.
Send them to trash and then delete ASAP.

Copy and paste to my memory
the documents from Your Word.
Hit save
that I may forward
to a world that is in need.
Let Your Word be my screensaver
that it is You I see
and when others read my texts,
it will be You they see.

A DISCIPLE

Through my faith and devotion
I walked on water,
but
I sank
not once, but thrice.
Still
He made me a shepherd
of His sheep
of His sheep
of His lambs
and
still He loved me.
I am Peter.

Robed and Ringed

At the end of my road,
I started back — no lower could I go.
Today my walk can be no slower,
my head can hang no lower
though I'd been down this road a thousand times before.
The stench of swine is still on my feet —
hog mud between my toes.
I'll ask to be a slave for that's the way it goes.

I hear the labored breathing —
he is running,
running to me.
I will explain that
a son I have no hope to be —
only a hired servant if he'll let me be.
But before I have a chance to get the words out,
he turns to the others and begins to shout.
He calls for the best robe,
the *best* robe for me.
For me, he is calling
for a robe and a ring.
They wash my feet
for a *feast* he is ordering.
The whole place is hopping.
Can this really be?
You see, my amazing father — he
though I don't deserve it —
though I am not worthy —
he is restoring sonship
in full measure to me.

The Question and the Answer

Pleased with her boys
James and John,
the mother asked the Lord
if they could sit in heaven
by His side adored
one on His left side
the other on His right
when He would become King
and rule in power and in might.

The answer came to her
with a question of His own —
"Can they bear the cross that I will bear —
the cross comes before the throne —
the burden of the shame
as I walk up Calvary
My mutilated body will be nailed upon
that loathsome tree?
Can they do the same?
Can they speak to others
when others turn away?
Can they love when hatred
surrounds them day by day?
When others spit upon them,
will they pray 'Forgive'?
You shall indeed drink the cup I drink
but these seats of honor are not Mine to give, you see,
My Father alone in heaven set aside
whose they will be."

WE EIGHT

We waited and we watched
and worked as best we could
as Noah built the ark
of the gopher wood.

Together board by board
and then pitched it with tar.
Then they began to come
two by two from afar.

When we were safe inside,
it was God who shut the door
the animals and eight of us —
eight and no more.

The rain washed away the sawdust
many screamed and cried outside
the ark lifted as the water rose
yet we were safe inside.

His Presence

I like to see the sun come up
over the rim of my coffee cup
and feel reborn to this new day.
My first choice is whether
I will bend my knees to pray.
Then, will I open my Bible to see
what message God has for me.
He is waiting to see my moves
He wants this day to go smooth.
He longs for me to feel His love and power
as I walk with Him each and every hour.
He wants my eyes to behold His glory
as I recall the old, old story
of His death on Calvary
to bring a world of peace to me.
Because He knows I am faulty and weak
He extends His hand for me to seek.
The darkness of my heart comes to face the Light of Day
when I truly obey and trust Him to guide my way.
On days when I am rushed and do not meet the Lord in prayer
I soon become worn out from my load of care.
My day is doomed, my peace cracked and shattered.
For I am only me, frail and fragile,
simple, weak — I forget what truly matters.
Useless, I am without Him
going to the battlefield exposed
having no protection for dealing with my foes.
Yesterday's garments will never do —
they must be made each day fresh and anew.
When arising from our time together
His armor on my back
I can go forth in any weather
for there is nothing that I lack.

I Wonder if Joseph Cried

I wonder if Joseph cried
as the image of his brothers grew
smaller and smaller in the distance until
they were only a speck on the horizon and
then nothing.
I wonder if Joseph cried.
Did he bury his face in the camel's hide
in that dusty caravan
and unleash the tears in the dust for the cruelty
his brothers had unleashed on him?

When he saw in his master Potiphar's face
that he believed his wife's cruel lies
and respect and honor turned to rage,
I wonder if Joseph cried.
Did he clutch the coat she'd left behind
and hold it to his face to catch the tears
in the stench of lust
that had been lashed at him?

When he, the dreamer and interpreter,
waited month after month for two long years
for the butler who'd been restored
to remember him
forgotten in a prison cell,
I wonder if Joseph cried.
Did he turn his face to the wall
and empty his heart of the tears inside?

For I know that Joseph cried
when they came bowing low as they could,
for they'd been forced to come for their livelihood.

They knew not it was he,
but he knew their faces well
and he heard Reuben say,
"Did I not tell you that day
'Do not sin against this child.'
Now his blood is required."

For I know that Joseph cried
when he saw his brother Ben again
and heard Judah say
that he himself would sell his own body away
rather than have Benjamin stay.

Joseph's tears washed away
all the hurt that there had been.
Forgiveness, wet with tears,
as with blood in days to come,
when the guilty world would hear the Lord say,
"Forgive them for they know not what they do."
"What you meant for evil
God meant for good for you" were Joseph's words too.
The plan of salvation required more than we could do.
Because of our sins, God sent Jesus to atone
for our salvation that we could not do alone.

Empty Mansions

We build our houses
just so, just so
we add on, re-do
just so, just so
we build them beautiful and
we build them grand,
we add the paint
just so, just so
it must be the exact hue
and then the fabric and the trim
and furniture and drapes and sconces and paintings
just so, just so,
but before we know
the houses begin to age
and the colors and furnishings,
and must be updated,
renovated, redecorated
just so, just so,
but no one seems to really see them
they never knew that we have lived in them
just so, just so
do we ourselves even know that we have lived
just so, just so
when we could have lived
justly so
for in His righteousness we could have lived
justly so,
and they would have seen our mansions
built by His design,
painted by His glory,
furnished with His works,
and they would have seen our mansions

and they would have known how to
build theirs for a lasting kingdom land
and not our own righteousness
which is sinking sand.

He Is Royalty

He is Royalty
and I am redeemed.
I am dependent
and He is divine.
He is my Father
and I am His child.
He is the Shepherd
and I am the sheep
He is Royalty
and I am redeemed.
He alone is our salvation.

The Sunday School Class That Isn't

The teacher of the phantom class
had heard excuses that were not new.
The teachers before him had all heard them too.
The teacher made personal visits,
phone calls galore,
letters and postcards
sent out by the score.
For several years he prayed continuously
studied lessons and taught to a class of one or two
before feeling like a failure and finding something else to do.
The excuses ranged
from the lame "overslept"
to the strong "had to work"
in between
"baby sick"
"me sick"
"went to visit"
"vacation"
"no car"
"he won't go"
"she won't go"
"bad hair day"
"nothing to wear"
"building a house."
One and the same
they go to and fro,
but to church, they do not go,
and the last time they will attend
they won't even know.

Glimpsing Glory

I caught a glimpse of glory,
floodgates opened wide —
God's riches in bountiful measure
waiting, waiting inside.
The storehouse full of blessings,
He wishes to bestow —
beauty exchanged for ashes —
if only to Him we go.
He is the Master of the storehouse.
He is waiting and wanting to bless.
He has a bountiful treasure —
true joy and happiness.
I felt His immediate blessing
flow to my heart and mind
as the floodgates began to open
and I possessed the treasures inside
that He gives to those who abide.
Oh, how He wants to give us
the bountiful treasures inside.

WORSHIPWISE

We worship the god of sex.
Sex cannot save us.
Look at the devastation —
men butcher women that they vowed to honor
adults buy children and then throw them away
men lust after men for a day.
The sex god's ways are wicked
and lead to death.

We worship the god of government.
Government cannot save us.
Look at the monstrous machine of the power hungry —
time, money, courts, judges, deceit, lies,
bribes, rights, suits
suits run through a wringer till
wrongs are rights and money might.
Governments shall fall.
The Word of the Lord will stand forever.

We worship the god of education.
Education cannot save us.
Look at the institutions of learning where children cannot pray
and God's law is outlawed
yet people picket and fight with all their might to teach that
man came from a monkey and abortion is okay.
Wisdom is trampled by educated fools
on their road to hell.

We worship the god of entertainment.
Entertainment cannot save us.
Look at the millions who worship in arenas everywhere
spending billions of dollars

for gold necklaces, chariots of dust, and dins of sin
for idols of entertainment
while Satan's entertainment is keeping score.
Entertainment scars would-be heroes
and their worshiping false fans.

We worship the god of religion.
Religion cannot save us.
Look at the false priests, preachers
the organized rules and regulations
that tie and bind and hypnotize
and mesmerize into total darkness
leaving out the one and only
Savior Jesus Christ who bled and died.
Religion will lead to decay
for only Jesus is the Way!

Tissue Paper

I am tissue paper.
I crumble easily.
I would be cast away quickly, but
You are there — an iron —
to press the wrinkles away
and make me like new.
Brand me
that I may show Your imprint
to a hungering world.

My Gift

Jesus,
it is Your world. You own it all.
What could I bring to Your manger stall?
Jesus,
to me You are dear.
What can I give You year after year?
Shepherds brought You their humble praise.
Wise men brought riches for Your eyes to gaze.
Jesus,
You are the world's treasure
You hold heaven's key.
Do You even require
a special gift from me?
For ages men have sung
regal songs to You.
Shall I sing a song too?
My voice by nature is weak and small.
I barely have a voice at all.
What shall I give of myself to You?
My Lord,
Is it enough that I simply bow right now
basking in the glory of the cradle and the cross
and give nothing back though a world is still lost?
What shall I give of myself to You?
Service to others that is true
and all of yourself every day of the year —
is that the answer from You I hear?

Prayer of Brotherhood

Lord,
help me hate
hate
and love
love.
Allow me,
Lord,
to taste
the agonies of every race.
In the stillness of their night,
instill in me their fright
as if it were my own.
Invest my vocal cords
when their voices sing
with vigor or savor laughter
as if it were my own.
Let me
not
hold debtor
death
when the day is done.
Brothers one
we shall have been
and at the end of day
will say
we could
we would
we did.

Am I Bigger Than That?

My sister and I had a little spat.
She refused to speak for weeks,
but am I bigger than that?

A woman at church laughed at my shoes.
I felt like saying, "Yours are uglier." What have I to lose —
but am I bigger than that?

Without stopping the neighbor's son ran over my cat.
I'd like to call him a selfish brat,
but am I bigger than that?

My husband said he's too busy to sit and chat.
I want to feel sorry for myself,
but am I bigger than that?

Our son off at college has forgotten where we're at.
Should we cut him out of the will,
or are we bigger than that?

I'm sick of death and dying
of pain and hurt and crying.
Some days I don't feel like trying
and want to shut myself away
"Who cares?" they seem to say.

Then Jesus gently reminds me
of the cross where He said, "I do.
In spite of it all, I care enough
that I gave My life for you."
No, I can never do better than that.

STAY AT IT

Stay at it
Stay at it
Stay at it
Stay at it

Stay at it
Stay at it
Stay at it
Stay at it

Stay at it
until it is done.
Stay at it
until you are done.
Life keeps on going
until your course is run.
When the roll is called,
you'll answer the first time —
no time left for finishing up —
no matter how long since you began
no matter what you have begun.
So stay at it
Stay at it
stay at it
stay
at
it.

Salvation

As we pray,
myself becomes
unraveled,
revealing
the core of
me,
humanity
entangled,
broken
before Holy God
who reveals Himself
knowing
caring
loving
showing mercy
forgiving
and lifting us up
setting us free
and pointing the way
for others to see
and fixing us —
reuniting us to Him
for eternity.

DAYS WITH JESUS

Days with Jesus
are the best days.
Life with Him
is complete.
A day with Jesus
must begin
on our knees
at Jesus' feet.

TOMORROW'S TOMORROW

One day the bell will toll for me.
They say it will, they do.
I am not sure there is a bell
but the meaning is still true.
The bell that beckons me
will bring a sweet release
from all life's troubles,
and my soul will know true peace.
Christ — He is my faith sufficient
to help me reach that goal
and exchange these burdens for a crown
to lay at Jesus' feet.

Times Get Tough, Lord

Times get tough
and we get weary,
Lord;
we don't always understand.
But we know
we will get through it,
Lord,
if You just hold our hand.

In Time of Trouble

If I were an alcoholic,
I'd imbibe.
If I were an addict,
I'd inject or pop a pill,
but
I am a Christian —
I'll trust and obey His will.

HE

When I was a child in a home of sin,
His Love nurtured me.
When I was a teen in a school of temptation,
His Word taught me.
When I was a young adult in a world of doubt,
His Light guided me.
When I was a busy parent in a chaos of activity,
His Spirit strengthened me.
I am certain as I go forth
in the uncertain years,
He will continue to calm all of my fears.
And on that day when I will lie on my crossing-over bed,
I'll be more alive than I could ever be dead.
As my view dims on this world,
His face will come into sight —
the One who guided my course on earth
will be with me on my heavenly flight.

When the World Trampled on Me

When the world trampled on
the best that I owned,
and I could not clearly see,
He held my hand as
I crawled along.
He led me to the tree —
the tree of Calvary —
the tree much higher than me.
He pointed my eyes upward
toward the skies to see
the tree much higher than me
the tree of Calvary —
where the blood flows down in love
all the way from the crown —
the blood of Christ
commissioned by God
His blood covering my sins once for all.
He helped me crawl until I could stand
by leading me to the tree
the tree that is higher than me
the tree of Calvary —

His Look from the Cross

His look from the cross —
oh, that look said it all
His look from the cross
His eyes saw the Father
His eyes saw me
He looked in love
from heaven to earth
from the Father to man
from the cross to me,
and His look said it all.
He was dying for me.

The Running Conversation

You say patience
when I say despair.
You say sacrifice
when I say rights.
You say forgive
when I say unfair.
You say go on
when I say quit.
Keep talking, Lord.
Please keep talking to me.

PRAYER FOR THE NEW YEAR

Lord,
We come to You fresh this morning —
well, no — not fresh —
left over from yesterday and yesteryear
and last night's celebrations
but Your mercies are fresh each morning.
We come to You to cleanse away
the eves, the yesterdays
and the yesteryears.
You know and understand
our broken promises
our shattered hopes
our empty dreams
our loneliness.
Many whom we loved of late are gone
and never will return to us
our babies who needed our tenderness
our children who needed our support
our youth who needed our guidance —
they are now adults who are as we once were —
giving and taking in love.
They do not need us now.
A world we do not know looms up
to laugh at the old
to shake a fist at wisdom
to mock God.
Come to us all, Lord, and reset our hearts
that we may grasp the God of All the Ages
who came to die for all generations
who came to love and show the way.
Help us now to span the bar
and not stand helpless as they crumble and fall

but, in spite of all, by our wisdom from You
to share their burdens
and lend our strength to their weakness
and accept their strength in our weakness.
In this new year help us to make new promises
to right the wrongs
to sing new songs
to create new dreams
and together lift our praise to You, O God on High,
who knows and cares and hears our cry.
Help us drink from one same cup
as we lift each other up.

Upon Receiving the News

From the backside of yesterday
in the bone of winter
a scrape against a nerve long asleep yawned and awoke
issuing on Facebook a post of primordial fear:
pray for me

And the backside of yesterday slid into morning sleeplessly
God, are You listening? Do You still know me?
Have I been away too long?
Have I misdialed inadvertently?

Praying
Praying for you
Praying you'll have peace
Praying fervently for you and family
On and on the posts

God, are You there?
Praying, praying for you
Praying you'll have healing
Praying for you and your family
On and on the posts

God, are You there?
"Child, do you not hear Me even yet?"

HE IS SUFFICIENT

The Lord has carried me
under His wings.
Now I know the strength
that only He brings.
That is the reason
my heart can still sing!

Grace, divine grace, was mine
on that day.
Through the valley of sorrow,
He led the way,
Carefully carrying me.
He was my stay!

Leaving the valley
and dark shadows behind,
God's grace greeted me
like bright sunshine.

Yes, His grace was for me
And His grace was free.

The measure of God's love
for you and for me
was His Son Jesus on Calvary's tree
And therein is grace
sufficient for me.

Grace to aid sorrow,
Grace full and free,
His grace is sufficient
for you and for me!

How Can I Be Saved?

- If you have never realized you are a sinner because of the sin of Adam, you need to come face to face with your separation from God by man's inborn sin.
  For all have sinned and fall short of the glory of God. (Romans 3:23)

- Ask God to forgive you and then turn from your sin.
  For the wages of sin is death, but the gift of God is eternal life in Christ Jesus our Lord. (Romans 6:23)

- Realize Jesus Christ is the ONLY way to be saved and ask Him to save you.
  For God loved the world in this way: He gave His one and only Son, so that everyone who believes in Him will not perish but have eternal life. (John 3:16)

- Tell someone you have accepted Jesus as your Savior and join a Bible-believing church for worship and Bible study.
  If you confess with your mouth, "Jesus is Lord," and believe in your heart that God raised Him from the dead, you will be saved. (Romans 10:9)

- Then begin a new lifestyle. Read the Bible and trust. Look at all the many promises God has given. Obey His command to put Him first and love others. Praise and thank Him often throughout the day.